Houses and Homes

Fiona Macdonald

W
FRANKLIN WATTS
NEW YORK • LONDON • SYDNEY

First published in 1998 by
Franklin Watts
96 Leonard Street
London EC2A 4RH

© Franklin Watts 1998

Franklin Watts Australia
14 Mars Road
Lane Cove
NSW 2006 Australia

Editor: Helen Lanz
Art Director: Robert Walster
Designer: Andy Stagg
Consultant: Saskia
Partington, Geffrye
Museum, London

ISBN 0 7496 3151 1
Dewey Decimal
Classification Number: 728

Printed in Malaysia

Picture Credits

Cover images: Mary Evans
Picture Library (main
image), Science and Society
Picture Library (bl),
Bubbles Photo Library/
Jenny Woodcock (br).

Interior: Bubbles Photo
Library p. 24tr; Mary Evans
Picture Library pp. 7, 10tr,
11t, 13t; Getty Images
pp. 8bl, 9t, 12, 21b, 23t, 23b,
26; Sally and Richard
Greenhill p. 21tl; Image
Bank p. 9br, 13br; London
Transport Museum pp. 20,
29b; National Energy
Foundation p. 27bl; National
Trust Photographic Library
pp. 14, 15t, 15b; Science and
Society Picture Library pp.
4, 6bl, 8tr, 18, 19t, 19b, 21br
22, 24bl, 25,27tr, 28tr, 29t;
Stock Market p. 6tr;
Franklin Watts/ P. Millard
pp. 3, 10bl, 11bl; Welwyn
Garden City Library pp. 16,
17t, 17b, 28bl.

CONTENTS

Introduction

People live in many different kinds of homes. Some are big houses, some are small flats. Some have gardens, others have not. Some people's homes are in the country, some people live in towns.

A house built in the 1990s.

Most houses today are comfortable and warm, but in the past, many houses were cold and damp.

This house from the 1930s does not have running water.

TIME LINE

1900s   1910s   1920s   1930s   1940s

This house was photographed in the 1890s, but it was built around 1800. Compare it with the modern house on page 6.

This book will tell you what houses were like in the past.

Look at this time line. It will tell you when the photographs showing the past were taken.

In the country

In the past, most people who lived in the country worked on farms nearby.

Some farms had small cottages on the land for the farmworkers to live in.

Bellows **pumped air to make the fire burn more brightly.**

Inside a farmworker's cottage around 1900. Can you see the bellows on the wall?

TIME LINE

1900s   1910s   1920s   1930s   1940s

A farmhouse in the 1900s.
The barns are behind the trees.

Farms also had stables, cattle-sheds and barns in their farmyards and on the land. Today, many of these farm buildings have been turned into new homes.

This old barn is now a house.

Housework

In the past, people had to do a lot of work to keep their homes clean and tidy.

Sweeping, polishing dusting, washing clothes and washing up dirty dishes all had to be done by hand. There were few machines to help.

This woman is using a *dolly peg*, a wooden tool to help her get the dirt out of her clothes.

In the early 1900s, many people used a washboard to rub their clothes against to get them clean.

TIME LINE

1900s   1910s   1920s   1930s   1940s

10

In this house, from around 1900, there are very many ornaments, such as clocks and vases, to clean and dust.

Polish like this was used to clean wooden floors and furniture to make them shine.

Upstairs, downstairs

In the past, rich people lived in big houses with many rooms. Each room was filled with beautiful furniture.

Servants lived in these big houses too. They worked hard to keep the houses clean.

This photograph shows a room full of furniture in a big house around 1910.

TIME LINE

1900s **1910s** 1920s 1930s 1940s

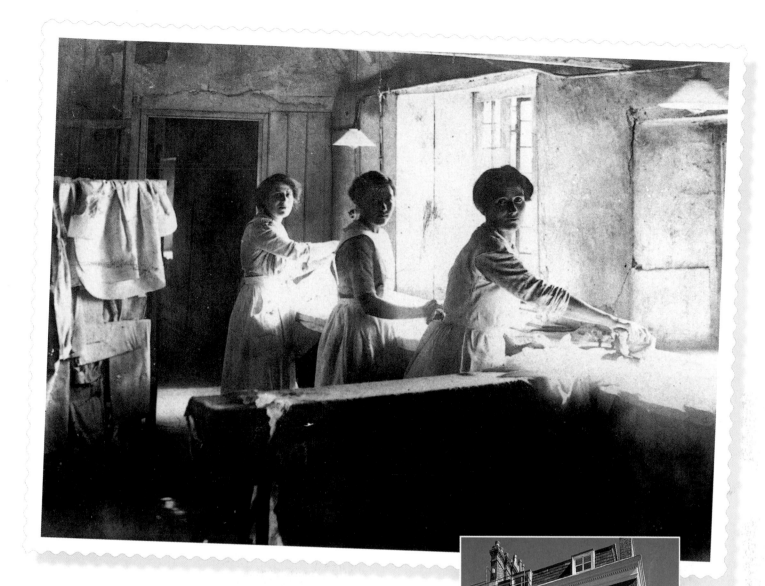

Servants worked in the *basement* rooms at the bottom of the house. They slept in the *attic* rooms, high up in the roof.

Today, many big houses have been divided into flats.

1950s   1960s   1970s   1980s   1990s   2000s

Stately homes

Stately homes are very old, and often very beautiful. They have hundreds of rooms and large gardens.

A kitchen in a stately home today, kept as it would have looked around 1910. Many servants worked here, cooking food for all the people living and working in the house.

Today, people can visit many stately homes. They can go on a guided tour to look at all the different rooms and the **antique** (old) furniture.

TIME LINE

1900s **1910s** 1920s 1930s 1940s

14

This photograph (above), from around 1910, was taken when a rich family lived in this stately home.

Today, no one lives here, but the house is open to visitors who can look round the many rooms.

Garden cities

As cities grew bigger, some people decided they would like to move away from crowded, noisy city streets.

So **garden cities** were developed. These were carefully planned to allow people to enjoy a healthy lifestyle, with many parks, gardens and open spaces.

In garden cities, outdoor areas were carefully *designed* and built at the same time as the houses and buildings.

TIME LINE

| 1900s | 1910s | **1920s** | 1930s | 1940s |

(Above) Houses in
Welwyn Garden City,
around 1920. The lane,
with its trees and
gardens, is still much
the same today (left).

City slums

A kitchen in a slum house, 1938. Compare this kitchen with the one on page 14.

In the past, many poor people lived in run-down houses called **slums**. There were lots of slums in big cities. They were damp and unhealthy. Slums often did not have a bath or toilet, some did not even have clean water.

The people who lived in slums caught many diseases. So, the government knocked a lot of them down, and built new homes to replace them. But there are still housing problems today.

TIME LINE

1900s   1910s   1920s   **1930s**   1940s

These children are playing in tumbled-down slums, 1934.

Families from slum areas were moved into new flats like these. These flats were built in 1937 to replace slum houses.

In the suburbs

In the 1920s and 1930s, many new houses were built on the outskirts of big cities. New roads, shops and schools were built there too. These new **communities** were called 'suburbs'.

This train time-table shows how the new railway service allowed people living in the suburbs (shown at the top of the picture) to travel to the city centre (shown at the bottom of the picture).

People living in the suburbs travelled to work in big cities on buses and trains.

TIME LINE

1900s   1910s   1920s   **1930s**   1940s

(Left) The suburbs today.
(Below) This house was built around 1930. Like many other houses in the suburbs, it is semi-detached (joined on one side to the house next door).

Homes for heroes

During the Second World War (which lasted from 1939 to 1945) many houses were destroyed by bombs. The government had to build new homes very quickly.

Families gather their belongings from the ruins of their bombed homes, 1940.

One way of building homes quickly was to make all the different parts – walls, windows, doors and roofs – in a factory.

TIME LINE

1900s	1910s	1920s	1930s	**1940s**

Fitting a house together, 1945.

The parts were then delivered to the building site, where builders fitted them together to make instant homes.

The finished houses were called *pre-fabs*.

Machines in the home

Today, most homes have machines, such as microwaves, ovens, fridges, freezers, vacuum cleaners and washing machines. These machines have changed the way people live and work at home.

Heating food in a microwave today. Microwaves cook food very fast.

Over the years, household machines, like the cookers on these pages, have been developed and improved in many ways.

This type of electric oven was widely used in the 1930s and 1940s.

TIME LINE

1900s   1910s   1920s   1930s   **1940s**

After the war the designs of cookers changed. This electric cooker was made in 1945. It looks much more modern than the one on page 24.

Towers and new towns

This tall block of flats was built in **1964**.

In the 1960s, many tall blocks of flats, called tower blocks, were built in big cities. But some people did not like living in such high buildings. They felt cut off from the streets below.

Today, many tower blocks have been replaced by smaller blocks of flats or new styles of housing.

Moving into a new town in the 1960s. The houses have only just been built.

(Below) Some new town houses test modern ideas today. This house uses the energy from the sun to heat it.

Also in the 1960s, some **new towns** were built in the countryside because old cities were becoming too crowded. New town houses were often built in very modern styles.

1950s **1960s** 1970s 1980s 1990s 2000s

Useful words

antique: old objects or furniture that are often valuable.

attic: a room at the top of a house, underneath the roof.

basement: rooms at the bottom of a house, below ground level.

bellows: a small, hand-powered pump for blowing air.

community: a group of people living in one area.

design: a drawing that shows how something should be made or how something should look.

dolly peg: a household tool made out of wood. It was used to move wet soapy washing around to drive out the dirt.

garden cities: new cities built to give the people who live there open spaces, such as parks and playgrounds, and lots of fresh air.

new towns: these are towns that were planned and built all at once in places that were farmland. Many were built in the 1950s and 1960s.

pre-fab: a house built from parts made in a factory, which can be fitted together on a building site.

slums: streets of damp, cold, run-down houses. Slums are usually found in big cities.

stately homes: big, old, splendid houses, built for lords and ladies, and other famous or powerful people.

suburbs: streets of comfortable houses built on the outskirts of cities. Many workers moved out of city centres to live in the suburbs.

Index